THE MASTER'S PLAN *for* VICTORY

Vic Reasoner

**2120 Culverson Ave
Evansville, IN 47714-4811**

© 2025 Victor Paul Reasoner
ISBN 979-8-9916819-7-1
Library of Congress Control Number: 2025945983

The Master's Plan for Victory

God does not have to win anything in order to remain sovereign. Tozer said a god less than sovereign would not bestow moral freedom upon his subjects. He would be afraid to do so. Yet our freedom does not overrule God's sovereignty.[1]

God does not need to protect his position or his reputation. He has nothing to hide or to fear. But motivated by love, he entered into a covenant partnership with humanity. We lost little time in gumming up the works. Yet he conceived a master plan to redeem our fallen race who was under the sentence of death. Without violating our freedom to choose — and that freedom was real, libertarian freedom incorporating the power of contrary choice — he maintains his sovereignty, executes justice, upholds his holiness, and demonstrates his magnanimous love, grace, and mercy.

We are so crippled by sin that we can do nothing to save ourselves, but the Spirit of God enables us to turn to God and trust in the substitutionary atonement of his Son. I have written about *The Possibilities of Full Salvation* (2025). But that book deals with salvation at a personal level. In this book, I want to try to explain

---

[1]Tozer, *Knowledge of the Holy*, 118. See also Lewis, *The Problem of Pain*, 117.

salvation at a cosmic level. God has a plan for world redemption, restoration, and revival.

The term *eschatology* is based on the Greek word *eschatos*, which means *last things*. Eschatology includes such fundamental doctrines as the second coming of Christ, the resurrection and judgment, heaven and hell. Eschatology is the study of God's plan for the establishment and victory of his church.

To the degree that we understand his plan and trust him, we can live in confidence. As we worship him, our lives can have purpose as his kingdom agents who make the crown rights of King Jesus our first priority. As we keep covenant with him, he can use us to advance his master plan on planet earth.

According to Acts 3:19-21 we are moving toward a time of *restoration* or *restitution*. A related word occurs in Matthew 19:28 and Titus 3:5. When it is used of individuals who have been born again, as in Titus 3:5, it is translated *regeneration*. When it is used of Christ's kingdom, as in Matthew 19:28, it is translated *renewal*.

How We Lost Hope

God's original purpose was for mankind to rule this world under him. He said, "Let us make man in our image, in our likeness, and let them rule." He declared, "Be fruitful and increase in number, fill the earth and subdue it. Rule over the fish of the sea and the birds of the air and over every living creature that moves on the ground" (Gen 1:26-28). This is often referred to as the cultural mandate — which defines our relationship with creation and nature. "You made him a little lower than the heavenly beings and crowned him with glory and honor. You made him ruler over the works of your hands;

you put everything under his feet" (Ps 8:5-6).

Dominion was at least part of the image of God in humanity. We were his viceregents. "The highest heavens belong to the Lord, but the earth he has given to man" (Ps 115:16).

But when Adam sinned, he brought the human race under the domain of darkness. In Adam all died. Death entered this world like a pandora's box which was opened. All the misery, pain, disease, and fighting that is in the world today was unleashed with their first sin. And the consequences of their sin have been passed on to all of their descendants — including us.

We lost our dominion over the earth. When we rebelled against God, nature rebelled against us. According to Romans 8:18-25, the entire creation was subjected to suffering through Adam's choice. The verb *was subjected* is in the passive voice, indicating that creation was implicated involuntarily.

When Adam and Eve sinned, they came under Satan's authority. Satan is not coequal with God, but he has a realm in which he rules. Whenever we willfully sin, we enter that realm and he establishes his stronghold in our life. Salvation is a transfer of ownership. When we are saved, God rescues us from the dominion of darkness and brings us into the kingdom of the Son (Col 1:13). Those who have not been saved are still under this dominion of darkness.

When our first parents sinned, they were banished from the garden of Eden and the tree of life, and the created order was broken. The curse of sin has been passed down to the entire human race from generation to generation. The serpent was cursed. The ground was cursed. The pain of childbirth was greatly increased. There would be a struggle for authority between husband and wife.

While Satan did not gain *ownership* of the world, since

the earth is the Lord's (Ps 24:1), he did gain *control* because we had been given control and were held hostage by him.

The devil's real agenda was to gain control of the world. Since Adam and Eve were left in charge and since they relinquished that authority to the devil, he claimed control by holding us hostage. He became the ruler of darkness of this world and the whole world was under the darkness of his occupation.

Oppressive dictatorships were the norm all across history. The Pharaohs of Egypt, the Assyrian kings, the Babylonian kings, the Medes and the Persians, the Greek monarch, and the Roman emperors all required worship and were all tyrants.

Daniel 2 describes four world empires as one idol, symbolizing their continuity. Daniel 7 also covers the same span of history, but instead of a shining metal icon, he saw carnivorous beasts — a lion, a bear, a leopard, and a monster — consuming everything that stood in their way.

Across thousands of years, mankind individually and collectively lived in bondage. But God loved humanity. By postponing Adam's punishment, God had to deal with Satan's claim. The world sat in darkness until Christ came. But with his coming a new day dawned (Rom 13:12).

The First Ray of Hope

The first promise that the kingdom of darkness would be crushed came immediately after the fall when God warned Satan, "I will put enmity between you and the woman, and between your offspring and hers; he will crush your head and you will strike his heel" (Gen 3:15). The Messiah would come through Abraham's lineage and more specifically through the virgin Mary. Her offspring, Jesus the Christ, would crush Satan.

Paul explained, "Death reigned from the time of Adam to the time of Moses" (Rom 5:14). Why did Paul select this segment of history? With the giving of the law to Moses, God established a covenant people.

With the giving of the law, the nation of Israel was chartered as God's visible kingdom on earth. While the world still sat in darkness, the light given to Israel was to spread to the whole world. Yet there were a few exceptional cases of those outside the nation of Israel who were included. Augustine has a chapter in the *City of God* entitled, "Whether before Christian times there were any outside of the Israelite race who belonged to the fellowship of the heavenly city."[2] In addition to Job, there were also Jethro and Melchizadek. Even Balaam had some revelation of the true God.

The Covenant with Abraham

Beginning with Abraham, God began to establish a visible kingdom on earth. God promised him, "I will bless those who bless you, and whoever curses you I will curse; and all peoples of the earth will be blessed through you" (Gen 12:3). This is the first statement of the covenant God made with Abraham. God gave him the astounding promise that, "all peoples on earth will be blessed through you." Later God told Abraham that his offspring would be more numerous than the stars in the sky and the sand on the seashore. His descendants would spread out in all four directions (Gen 28:14).

Two thousand years after the promise was made to Abraham it was fulfilled in Jesus Christ, the seed of Abraham (Gal 3:16). John describes a multitude in heaven so great that no one can count them (Rev 7:9), comprising every nation, lan-

---

[2]Augustine, *City of God*, *NPNF*1 2:389-90.

guage, and culture. These are the *stars* and *sand* promised Abraham. This kingdom had a small beginning, in fact so small that Jesus referred to it as a mustard seed (Matt 13:31-32). Yet it will grow into a great tree which has great influence and blessing.

Jacob's Blessing

If we listen while Jacob blesses his sons, we will hear a promise that has global implications. Jacob describes the Messiah as a ruler whose kingdom would extend beyond Israel to other nations. There is a hint of the universal reign of Christ in *the obedience of the nations* in Genesis 49:10. Even Balaam catches a glimpse of this rule in Numbers 24:17-19. Micah said that after the ruler came, his greatness would reach the ends of the earth (5:2-4).

This prophecy of Jacob predicted the expansion of Christ's kingdom on the basis of his atonement. As we visit other mountain peaks, this view will come into sharper focus. But even when the "nation" of Israel consisted of only twelve sons, an international kingdom was foretold.

A Nation of Priests to the World

Just before Moses was given the ten commandments at Mount Sinai, God revealed his plan for world evangelism.

> Now if you obey me fully and keep my covenant, then out of all nations you will be my treasured possession. Although the whole earth is mine, you will be for me a kingdom of priests and a holy nation (Exod 19:5)

God claimed the whole world as his own. "The earth is the Lord's, and everything in it, the world, and all who live in it" (Ps 24:1) and the glory of the Lord fills the whole earth (Num 14:21). However, the world was in darkness and Israel was to be a kingdom of priests and a holy nation. Just as one tribe, the tribe of Levi, served as priests for Israel, so the entire nation was to serve as priests for the world.

The condition was that Israel must obey fully the law of God. As they kept covenant with God, they would become an example to the world. While Israel failed to evangelize her world, God's plan was not thwarted. Under the new covenant the church becomes the Israel of God. Peter picks up this language used by God in Exodus 19 in 1 Peter 2:9.[3]

The Year of Jubilee

Leviticus 25 declared every forty-ninth year as a year of jubilee. Debts were canceled, property was returned, and freedom was restored. The year of jubilee looks back to deliverance from Egyptian bondage and looks ahead to the final redemption by the Messiah. Isaiah wrote,

> The Spirit of the Sovereign Lord is on me, because the Lord has anointed me to preach good news to the poor. He has sent me to bind up the brokenhearted, to proclaim freedom for the captives and release from darkness for the prisoners, to proclaim the year of the Lord's favor (61:1-2).

Jesus began his public ministry by reading these words and announcing that he was the fulfillment of Isaiah's prophecy

---

[3]Reasoner, *1-2 Peter*, 87-92.

(Luke 4:18-21).

This jubilee mandate has world implications. In Luke 4, Jesus declared that it began with his first advent. It will be completed by his second coming, "the restitution of all things" (Acts 3:21). Between Christ's first and second advent, between Christ's first advent and ascension back to heaven and his second advent when he comes from heaven to raise the dead and judge the world — this restoration is being accomplished progressively. It is the new creation described in Isaiah 65:17-25.

Adam Clarke understood this restoration to correspond to the Year of Jubilee which began at Christ's first advent. This "year" lasts until all things prophesied regarding the kingdom of God have been restored. Then Christ returns after the kingdom of God has been restored.[4]

The new heaven and new earth in Isaiah 65:17 is descriptive of the gospel age. Death, however, has not yet been conquered (v 20). In Isaiah's description, the kingdom of God on earth has produced a new world, but not a perfect world.

In 2 Peter 3:13 the new heavens and a new earth which comes *after* the return of Christ (v 12) and the final judgment.

In Revelation 21-22 John saw a new heaven and a new earth, but there will be no more death (21:4) and no more curse (22:3). This condition also comes *after* the return of Christ and final judgment at the end of chapter 20. Therefore, neither 2 Peter 3 nor Revelation 21-22 can properly be used to understand the nature of present kingdom.

However, Clarke explained that this *new* earth in Isaiah

---

[4]Clarke, *Commentary*, 5:707.

65:17 refers ultimately to the full conversion of the Jews.[5] Thomas Coke wrote that the expressions in Isaiah 65

> signify a new and better form of religion, to be introduced into the church, the old and inferior one being abolished. It is plain, from what follows, that the prophet here foretells a future and highly-improved state of religion and felicity, greater than has yet been experienced in the church of Christ.[6]

Amos Binney also noted the contrast between Isaiah 65/ 2 Peter 3 and Revelation 21.[7] Rather than creating confusion, this contrast illustrates the kingdom principle of already/not yet. At the level of personal salvation there is a relative Christian perfection available in this life, but only in heaven will saints reach full perfection. In a similar way we can see great advancement of Christ's kingdom here on earth, but heaven alone provides full and perfect redemption.

Resurrection Power

Although the books following the Pentateuch are historical records, in the Psalms David anticipated the resurrection and session of Christ in Psalm 2. The nations rage and Satan roars, but God laughs in scorn at all humanistic conspiracies to usurp his master plan. Their rebellion against him is specifically directed against his Anointed One. The Hebrew word for *anointed* is *mashiach* (Messiah); the Greek equivalent is

---

[5]Clarke, *Commentary*, 4:240.

[6]Coke, *Commentary*, 3:751.

[7]Binney, *Commentary*, 702.

christos (Christ). No name is any more hated by the world than Lord Jesus Christ.

But God is undaunted. He has installed Christ as King. The inauguration of Christ occurred after his resurrection. Although the text, "You are my Son; today I have become your Father" is often misused by false teachers to prove Jesus was a created being, Acts 13:33 demonstrates that this verse describes the resurrection, not the supposed creation, of Jesus Christ.

The writer of Hebrews puts the verse into its correct context. "After he had provided purification for sins, he sat down at the right hand of the Majesty in heaven." He became superior to the angels, for "to which of the angels did God ever say, 'You are my Son; today I have become your Father?'" (Heb 1:3b-5). The *today* of Psalm 2:7 pinpoints the resurrection of Christ as the time he became king. His kingdom was not postponed.

At the coronation of Christ as king, the Father gave his Son an inaugural gift. He decreed, "Ask of me, and I will make the nations your inheritance, the ends of the earth your possession. You will rule them with an iron scepter; you will dash them to pieces like pottery" (vv 7-9). The Father has given the Son the nations for his inheritance and the ends of the earth for his possession. All human conspiracies will fail because God has predestined his own plan.

Atonement and Dominion

Psalm 22 begins with the words Jesus used on the cross, "My God, my God, why have you forsaken me?" It describes the suffering of the Messiah, but not his abandonment. Then it ends on a climatic note portrays the victory of Christ through his atoning death.

All the ends of the earth will remember and turn to the Lord, and all the families of the nations will bow down before him, for dominion belongs to the Lord and he rules over the nations. All the rich of the earth will feast and worship; all who go down to the dust will kneel before him — those who cannot keep themselves alive. Posterity will serve him; future generations will be told about the Lord. They will proclaim his righteousness to a people yet unborn — for he has done it (vv 27-31).

This gospel will be passed down from one generation to the next. "One generation will commend your works to another; they will tell of your mighty acts" (Ps 145:4). The ultimate result of Christ's sufferings is that his church will extend to the whole earth. "All the ends of the earth will remember and turn to the Lord."

Sovereign Over Heaven and Earth

Psalm 24 begins with the declaration that the earth is the Lord's. This world has never belonged to Satan. "For God is the King of all the earth" (Ps 47:7).

Then the scene shifts from earth to heaven. The "hill of the Lord" is identified in Psalm 2:6 as Zion. Originally David had sung the words of this psalm as he carried the ark of the covenant back to Jerusalem. There actually was a Jerusalem gate known as *Zion Gate*. As David ascended to Jerusalem, no doubt he called to the gatekeeper to open the gates that he might enter with the ark.

We, too, are on a journey — a journey from earth to heaven. We are marching to Zion. "You have come to Mount Zion, to the heavenly Jerusalem, the city of the living God.

You have come to thousands upon thousands of angels in joyful assembly to the church of the firstborn, whose names are written in heaven" (Heb 12:22-23).

We are in the kingdom of Christ because we have acknowledged Christ as our king. The closing verses of this psalm apply to the ascension of Christ. He returned to heaven after the resurrection as the king of glory. Therefore, Christ is in control in heaven and on earth. "Yet at present," the writer of Hebrews explains, "we do not see everything subject to him" (Heb 2:8). However, the implication of this psalm is that those who keep covenant with their Savior seek his face and in turn he blesses them. The church then becomes the channel of blessing through which Christ the king blesses the earth and brings it under his dominion. The same king who is recognized in heaven will someday be recognized as sovereign on earth.

A Prosperous Kingdom

Psalm 72 provides a beautiful description of that period when the kingdom of God covers the earth.

> He will defend the afflicted among the people and save the children of the needy; he will crush the oppressor. He will endure as long as the sun, as long as the moon, through all generations. He will be like rain falling on a mown field, like showers watering the earth. In his days the righteous will flourish; prosperity will abound till the moon is no more. He will rule from sea to sea and from the River to the ends of the earth (vv 4-8).

The last phrase "from the River to the ends of the earth"

was also used in Zechariah 9:10. This is a reference to the Euphrates River. This, then, is a reference to the cradle of civilization which was located between the Tigris and Euphrates Rivers. From this beginning point, the kingdom will spread to become a universal kingdom. "All the nations you have made will come and worship before you, O Lord" (Ps 86:9).

The Session of Christ

Christ reigns and will reign until he has put all enemies under his feet. The period between his first and second advent is the period of Christ's victorious rule. That he reigns in heaven is an undisputed fact. But Paul tells us in 1 Corinthians 15:22-27 that there is a progressive conquest in which every dominion, authority, and power is destroyed — culminating in death itself. Since Christ has no rival in heaven and since death cannot enter heaven, this reign of Christ must also be extended to earth.

Psalm 110:1 is quoted in the New Testament more frequently than any other Old Testament verse. It is quoted or alluded to 23 times in the New Testament. It is quoted in eleven of the 27 New Testament books and by seven of the nine New Testament authors."The Lord says to my Lord: 'Sit at my right hand until I make your enemies a footstool for your feet,'" therefore is fundamental to New Testament eschatology.

Jesus claimed this was a reference to himself in Luke 22:69. In Acts 2 Peter explained the significance of Pentecost was that Jesus had been resurrected, he had ascended to the right hand of God where he was made Lord, and he had poured out the Holy Spirit as proof of his lordship. In the context (v 34) Peter also cites Psalm 110:1.

This, then, describes the present work of Jesus Christ. He is seated upon the throne of universal authority and has been since his resurrection and session. By faith we accept the teaching of scripture that everything will someday be brought under the lordship of Christ. "In putting everything under him, God left nothing that is not subject to him. Yet at present we do not see everything subject to him" (Heb 2:8). Jesus Christ legally rules this world *de jure*, although not yet *de facto*. This is the eschatological tension between the already and the not yet.

Paul said, "He must reign until he has put all his enemies under his feet. The last enemy to be destroyed is death." He will hand the kingdom over to the Father after he "has destroyed all dominion, authority and power" (1 Cor 15:24-26).

This means that Christ will not return to rescue a defeated church. He sits on his throne in heaven *until* the battle is won. The church is fully equipped to finish the fight.

Since Christ is omnipresent, his physical location is relatively unimportant. Christ rules from the heavenly Zion (v 2). John Jefferson Davis grasped this concept when he wrote,

> Christ remains in heaven while his foes are being subdued and until that process is complete.... Christ does not need to be physically present on earth to subdue his spiritual foes; this he does while still at the Father's right hand in heaven.[8]

He will reign on his heavenly throne until every earthly challenge to his authority has been put down. Only then will he return. Those who refer to Christ as the *coming* king only have it half right. He is the king *now*. Christ has all authority,

---

[8] Davis, *Christ's Victorious Kingdom*, 33.

power, and dominion in this present age, as well as in the one to come. And he shares that authority with his church.

A Peaceful Kingdom

The prophets anticipated the worldwide success of God's kingdom. Isaiah said,

> In the *last days* the mountain of the Lord's temple will be established as chief among the mountains; it will be raised above the hills, and all nations will stream to it. Many peoples will come and say, "Come, let us go up to the mountain of the Lord, to the house of the God of Jacob. He will teach us his ways, so that we may walk in his paths." The law will go out from Zion, the word of the Lord from Jerusalem. He will judge between the nations and will settle disputes for many peoples. They will beat their swords into plowshares and their spears into pruning hooks. Nation will not take up sword against nation, nor will they train for war anymore (2:2-4).

Last days refers to the period of time after Christ came the first time and before he comes again. The phrase "in the days to come" or "in the later days" occurs fifteen times in the Old Testament. In none of the passages does it refer to the end of time. The writer of Hebrews began by saying that in the past God spoke at many times and various ways, "but in these *last days* he has spoken to us by his Son" (Heb 1:2). There this description, and the parallel passage in Micah 4:1-3, describe a condition which will be fulfilled in the period between the first and second advent of Christ.

While part of Isaiah 2:4 is on a wall at the United Nations building, world peace will not come through career diplomats. The immediate context in Isaiah suggests that it is as nations are converted and worship the same God and are instructed in his law, that peace comes.

"The earth will be full of the knowledge of the Lord as the waters cover the sea" (Isa 11:9) and the result of that knowledge is world peace. Only through Jesus Christ can ancient hostilities be put to death (Eph 2:14-16).

Isaiah continues in 19:19-25 by foretelling a day when both Arab and Jew will worship together. Arabs will not embrace Judaism nor will Jews convert to Islam. Instead, both will discover that Christ is the Savior of the world. We are specifically told in Romans 11:26 that all Israel shall be saved and, since God does not show favoritism (Acts 10:34), we can reasonably assume that the Arab world will find peace from the same source.

Psalm 87:4 also describes ancient enemies who become part of Zion, "regenerated into the church of God."[9] Thus, the picture in Isaiah 35 of the desert blossoming depicts the inward change that takes place in the redeemed soul. Adam Clarke saw in this word picture "the flourishing state of the Church of God" through the "greater influence and extension of the Christian faith."[10]

The Birth of the King

Isaiah continued to explain that the birth of the Messiah meant the establishment and increase of the kingdom of God.

---

[9]Spurgeon, *The Treasury of David*, 4:116.

[10]Clarke, *Commentary*, 4:144.

> For to us a child is born, to us a son is given, and the government will be on his shoulders. And he will be called Wonderful Counselor, Mighty God, Everlasting Father, Prince of Peace. Of the increase of his government and peace there will be no end. He will reign on David's throne and over his kingdom, establishing and upholding it with justice and righteousness from that time on and forever (9:6-7).

David was promised that one of his own descendants would sit on his throne forever (Ps 132:11-12). The first fact established in the New Testament is that Jesus Christ is the son of David (Matt 1:1).

Yet unless the kingdom of Christ was established at his first advent, there has been no one sitting of David's throne for some two thousand years. While the promise made to David was conditional (Ps 89:39; 132:12), Amos 9:11-12 promised that David's fallen tent would be restored. And on the day of Pentecost, Peter explained that after Jesus was resurrected and exalted to the Father's right hand, he fulfilled the oath that God had made to David that one of his descendants would be on the throne (Acts 2:22-36).

This passage in Isaiah indicates the time at which Christ's kingdom will be established. "From that time on and forever" refers to the birth of Christ. At the time in which Christ is born, the light of a new day dawns (v 2; see Matt 4:16).

Isaiah also specifies the duration of this kingdom. Once established, it will never end. This suggests that the reign of Christ is not limited to a literal thousand years.

It is also significant that this government of peace increases (v 7) from the time of its beginning at the first advent. Just as the child who was born grows to maturity, so his kingdom "increases, and is daily more and more extended, and will continue till all things are put under his feet," according to Adam Clarke.[11]

The Atonement Brings Kingdom Growth

Isaiah also foresaw the suffering of the Messiah in chapter 53. Because Christ took our place and satisfied the justice of God, many will be justified. Since he was victorious over Satan, his spoils will be great. Commenting on v 12, J. Marcellus Kik wrote, "Who would dare to say that Christ's portion will be less than the devil's!"[12]

While there was a period of time when few were entering the kingdom, Isaiah predicted that after atonement the barren woman who had never bore a child would bear so many children the house would need to be enlarged! "Enlarge the place of your tent, stretch your tent curtains wide, do not hold back; lengthen your cords, strengthen your stakes. For you will spread out to the right and to the left" (Isa 54:2-3a). The father of modern missions, William Carey preached his famous sermon, "Expect great things from God. Attempt great things for God," from these verses.[13]

While Israel was married to God, she never bore any children. Israel made little attempt to evangelize the gentile world. Jonah was the only Old Testament missionary and he was a very reluctant one. But the kingdom of God could not be reduced to the state of Israel. Isaiah said the desolate woman would bear more children than the married woman.

---

[11]Clarke, *Commentary*, 4:65.

[12]Kik, *An Eschatology of Victory*, 27.

[13]Murray, *The Puritan Hope*, 139.

This is a reference to the new covenant.

Paul taught that Abraham's two wives symbolized two covenants. He then quotes Isaiah 54:1 to teach that there will be more children born under the new covenant than had been born under Judaism (Gal 4:24-31).

Therefore the church declares the call of God, "Turn to me and be saved, all you ends of the earth; for I am God, and there is no other. . . . Before me every knee will bow; by me every tongue will swear" (Isa 45:22-3).

In 25:6-9 and again in 49:6, Isaiah extends salvation to the ends of the earth. God intends to rule over the whole earth and foreigners are invited to participate in that kingdom.

A New World

Isaiah's vision of the coming kingdom reaches its zenith in chapter 65. Although vv 17-25 speak of creating new heavens and a new earth, it is clear that this is not a reference to the eternal state since death is still part of this world (v 20). Yet life expectancy will be lengthened. It will be a time of peace and prosperity. It is clear that this period in human history has not yet arrived. It is also clear that, although this is the first scriptural reference to new heavens and new earth, it refers to long life, not eternal life.

The Expanding River of Salvation

Ezekiel saw this coming kingdom as a river flowing from the temple (47:1-12). After the crucifixion of Christ and the giving of the Holy Spirit at Pentecost, God's Spirit would flow as a stream of living water from within (John 7:37-39). This prediction was made by Jesus Christ while in the old temple. A generation later that temple was destroyed. Paul taught that we are now God's temple and that God's Spirit lives in us (1 Cor 3:16-17). Therefore, Ezekiel 40-42 is not giving the exact measurements of a future rebuilt temple.

Today the river of the water of life flows from the throne of God and of the Lamb (Rev 22:1). The Spirit could not be given until Christ came and made atonement. The river of the Spirit flows from the cross. Believers drink that living water (John 4:10).

Ezekiel said at first this stream was ankle deep. Soon it became knee deep, then waist deep, and finally too deep to measure. This growth is not natural. No river would naturally increase unless tributaries dumped into it. In contrast, this river will continue to expand over the passage of time. Ezekiel prophesied that at a point in time the fresh water will flow into the Dead Sea transforming it to fresh water and bringing it back to life. This symbolizes the transforming effect the kingdom of God will have upon the entire world. God will flood this world with his Spirit and bring healing to the nations (v 12; Rev 22:2).

It is this same Spirit which brings life to the famous valley of dry bones, described in Ezekiel 37:1-14, and creates a vast spiritual army. Spiritual resurrection or regeneration is described in John 5:24-27. Spiritual resurrection out of the dead is also described in Romans 6:13 and Ephesians 5:14; Colossians 2:13 says as much, but does not use the same wording.

Greg Beale connected John 5:24-29 and Romans 6:4-13 with Revelation 20:4-6, demonstrating that in each context physical and spiritual resurrection are described in the same immediate context.[14] The same Greek word used in Revelation 20:4 is used in the Septuagint, the Greek Old Testament,

---

[14]Beale, *NIGTC*, 1004-1013.

in Ezekiel 37:10. The church will see great revival when all Israel is saved. Romans 11 reveals that Israel will be regrafted as part of the church, the Israel of God (Gal 6:16).

The Kingdom Timetable

Daniel outlined four humanistic world empires: Babylonian, Medo-Persian, Greek, and Roman. In Daniel 2 these world empires are seen from an earthly perspective as something glamorous. In Daniel 7 the same outline is seen from a heavenly perspective and it is hideous.

> In the time of those kings, the God of heaven will set up a kingdom that will never be destroyed, nor will it be left to another people. It will crush all those kingdoms and bring them to an end, but it will itself endure forever (2:44).

Since the four world kingdoms did not exist simultaneously, but in sequence, it would be during the time of the last earthly kingdom, the Roman Empire, that the kingdom of God would be established. Once the kingdom of God is established there will be not reversal back to the kingdoms of man. There will be no revived Roman empire. And without a humanistic empire there can be no future antichrist world ruler. The term *antichrist* is only used five times: 1 John 2:18 (twice); 2:22; 4:3; 2 John 7. John describes something quite different from pop "left behind" theology. "*Antichrist* is "any *person, thing, doctrine, system of religion, polity*, &c, which is *opposed* to *Christ*, and to the spirit and spread of his Gospel."[15]

---

[15]Clarke, *Commentary*, 6:909.

The rock in Daniel's first vision is the kingdom of Christ according to v 44. This rock became a huge mountain and filled the whole earth, indicating the growth of the kingdom over time.

In Matthew 26:64 Jesus identified himself as the Son of Man of Daniel 7:13. Daniel 7:13-14 describes the ascension of Jesus as he returns to heaven. Christ approached the Ancient of Days and was given

> authority, glory and sovereign power; all peoples, nations and men of every language worshiped him. His dominion is an everlasting dominion that will not pass away, and his kingdom is one that will never be destroyed.

At the time of the ascension, the Ancient of Days was seated, court was in session, and the books were opened. Satan was stripped of any legal standing, and Christ was given an everlasting kingdom including all nations. Daniel 7:22-27 reveals that Satan's claim was thrown out of court and authority was handed over to the saints.

The Ancient of Days ruled in favor of Christ and against the claims of Satan. Satan continued to try to stop the church, but he has no legal standing. According to Revelation 12:12 he knows that he is running out of time for the judgment to be executed.

Countdown to the Kingdom

Daniel becomes even more exact in Daniel 9:24-27. Because Israel did not keep the seventh day, they went into Babylonian captivity for seventy years. While in captivity Daniel read in Jeremiah 29:10 that the captivity would last seventy years. He began seeking to understand God's plan regarding the rebuilding of Jerusalem and God revealed to Daniel a bigger plan. In "seventy sevens" or 490 years Jerusalem would be rebuilt, the Messiah would come and establish his kingdom, and Jerusalem would be torn down. During this period of time Christ the ruler came to establish his kingdom.

The Jews had been in captivity for seventy years. Now Daniel is told what would occur during *seventy sevens*. *Weeks* is actually not in the Hebrew text, but seven days equals a week. The context (9:1-2) refers to seventy years, so this period, revealed to Daniel, is seventy years times seven years.

- From the decree of Artaxerxes in 457 BC to rebuild the walls (Ezra 7) to the actual completion of the walls, streets, and moats (Dan 9:25) in 408 BC is a period of 49 years.

- From 408 BC to the Messiah is a span of 434 years. This is the inter-testamental period.

- Jesus began his public ministry in AD 27. That leaves one *week* of seven years remaining. After the 69th week, in the middle of the 70th week (after 3½ years of public ministry) the Messiah is cut off. His crucifixion put an end to sacrifice and offering. But his rejection as Messiah sealed the doom of the Jewish people. Jerusalem was under siege for 3½ years. The tribulation of those days was so severe Jesus warned that it was unequaled from the beginning of the world until the time Jesus spoke the warning "and never to be equaled again" (Matt 24:21).

Daniel saw this period of 490 years as a unit or block of time. In fact, although the term *seventy sevens* is plural, the verb is singular — seventy weeks *is* decreed. There is no gap between week 69 and week 70. According to v 26 this desolation was decreed within the 490-year unit. While the sentence was pronounced, it was not executed until forty years later. God, in his mercy, gave Israel one generation to repent.[16]

The Early and Later Rain

The Old Testament prophets also predicted an early and later rain of the Spirit. James upholds the example of the patient farmer, who waits for the early and later rain, as an example to all Christians (5:7). Hosea promised, "As surely as the sun rises, he will appear; he will come to us like the winter [later] rains, like the spring [former] rains that water the earth" (6:3).

As Joel prophesied concerning Pentecost, he also exclaimed, "Be glad, people of Zion, rejoice in the Lord your God, for he has given you the autumn rains because he is faithful. He sends you abundant showers, both autumn and spring rains" (2:23). Zechariah also encourages us to "ask for rain" (10:1).

The famous Bible commentator Matthew Henry (1662-1714) observed, "When God intends great mercy for his

---

[16]Because dispensationalists see the establishment of Christ's kingdom as a future event, they are forced to put a gap between the 69th and 70th week of at least 2000 years duration. This is unlikely since there was no gap between the first 7 weeks and the next 62 weeks. The burden of proof is theirs to explain why there would be an undetermined period of time within a determined period of time. The unmeasured gap is at least four times as long as the measured period. Or to say this 70th week is an undetermined length, perhaps 2000 years, contradicts the dispensational insistence upon a literal hermeneutic.

people the first thing he does is to set them a praying."[17] Jonathan Edwards wrote after the first great awakening, "When God has something very great to accomplish for his church, it is his will that there should precede it the extraordinary prayers of his people."[18]

The early rain was needed so that the planted seed would germinate. The latter rain was necessary for the plant to fill out and produce fruit. The purpose of the latter rain is to guarantee an abundant harvest. Just as Pentecost was the early rain which established the kingdom, the latter rain, which we are to pray for, will produce a great end time harvest of souls. "In that day the mountains will drip with new wine, and the hills will flow with milk; all the ravines of Judah will run with water. A fountain will flow out of the Lord's house and will water the valley of acacias" (Joel 3:18).

Pentecost was the early rain. Peter declared in Acts 3:19 that "times of refreshing may come from the Lord." Between the early and later rain, there may be many times of revival. Jonathan Edwards wrote,

> God has had it much on his heart, from all eternity, to glorify his dear and only-begotten Son; and there are some special seasons that he appoints to that end, wherein he comes forth with omnipotent power to fulfill his promise and his oath to him. Now these times are remarkable pouring out of his Spirit to advance his kingdom; such is a day of his power.[19]

---

[17] Henry, *Commentary*, 4:1462; notes on Zech 12:10.

[18] Edwards, *Edwards on Revivals*, 394-395.

[19] Edwards, *Works*, 4:126.

If Pentecost was the early rain, the Holy Spirit will also bring the latter rain. In fact, Hosea said this hope is as sure as the sunrise (6:3). Habakkuk declared, "The earth will be filled with the knowledge of the glory of the Lord, as the waters cover the sea" (2:14).

Another Picture of Peace

In the last days the mountain of the Lord's temple will be established as chief among the mountains; it will be raised above the hills, and peoples will stream to it. Many nations will come and say, "Come, let us go up to the mountain of the Lord, to the house of the God of Jacob. He will teach us his ways, so that we may walk in his paths." The law will go out from Zion, the word of the Lord from Jerusalem. He will judge between many peoples and will settle disputes for strong nations far and wide. They will beat their swords into plowshares and their spears into pruning-hooks. Nation will not take up sword against nation, nor will they train for war anymore. Every man will sit under his own vine and under his own fig tree, and no one will make them afraid, for the Lord Almighty has spoken. All the nations may walk in the name of their gods; we will walk in the name of the Lord our God for ever and ever (Mic 4:1-5).

The *last days* began with the coming of Christ and the establishment of his kingdom. Micah repeats the prophecy of Isaiah 2 concerning the peace which the kingdom of God will bring. The nations will flow into Zion.

Micah's references to the *mountain* or *Jerusalem, the*

house of God, the Lord's temple, and *Zion* are references to the church. Jesus Christ is the cornerstone laid in Zion (1 Pet 2:6). Zion is described as a mountain seven times in the New Testament. Hebrews 12 describes the church as a mountain to emphasize permanence. Zion is built upon Jesus Christ, the cornerstone, and those who do not believe in him do not belong to Zion. Thus, the church is Mount Zion, the heavenly Jerusalem.[20]

However, the church does not constitute the kingdom. Rather, it is an important part of it. Christ should be lord of every sphere of society — family, education, medicine, media, the arts, entertainment, business, and politics. God ordained three covenant institutions: the family, the church, and the state. He is above them all and relates to us through them. Any institution which is not built upon him and his truth will collapse.

Hebrews 12:18-29 warns that God's voice shook the earth when the law was given and God will shake this world again. John Wesley noted that this universal shaking began at the first coming of Christ and will be consummated at his second coming.[21] Everything which does not conform to God's kingdom plan will be leveled, but we are participants in a kingdom that cannot be shaken (Heb 12:28). Neither earthquake nor fire can destroy this kingdom!

The church is also portrayed as a city to emphasize presence. The church is the dwelling place of God. Therefore, when Micah states that "the Lord will rule over them in Mount Zion from that day and forever" (4:7), we need not conclude that Christ will physically reign forever from Jerusa-

---

[20]Reasoner, *Hebrews*, 200-207.

[21]Wesley, *Notes,* 593.

lem.

Then Micah adds that when this kingdom brings peace on earth, "Every man will sit under his own vine and under his own fig tree and no one will make them afraid" (4:4).

Zechariah adds that "men and women of ripe old age will sit in the streets of Jerusalem, each with cane in hand because of his age. The city streets will be filled with boys and girls playing there" (8:4-5).

The King's Arrival

Zechariah 9:9 described the Messiah entering Jerusalem on a donkey and then said, "He will proclaim peace to the nations. His rule will extend from sea to sea and from the River to the ends of the earth" (9:10b). A week before his resurrection Jesus did enter Jerusalem on a donkey in fulfillment of Zechariah's prediction (Matt 21:4-5). Therefore, the rule of Christ began at the time of his passion and triumph.

Zechariah 14 describes the siege of Jerusalem in AD 70. As the Christians fled, they carried the gospel with them and the water of salvation flowed out of Jerusalem so that the Lord becomes the king of all the earth (v 9).

The Old Testament closes with the anticipation of a coming kingdom. The New Testament opens with the good news that God has acted and that the kingdom is here. John Bright has written,

> To acclaim anyone as Messiah is to announce in him the coming of the Kingdom of God, for it is precisely the business of the Messiah to establish the Kingdom. Messiah cannot be separated from King-

dom.[22]

The Kingdom in the Gospels

The birth of Jesus Christ was the dawn of a great light to those who had lived in darkness (Matt 4:16). He came to bring peace on earth (Luke 2:14). John declared, in his prologue, that the light shines in the darkness and that the darkness is unable to overpower the light (John 1:5). Because light is more powerful than darkness, the kingdom of light will conquer the kingdom of darkness. Therefore John could write, "The darkness is passing and the true light is already shining" (1 John 2:8).

John the Baptist was the herald of the kingdom. He introduced Jesus by declaring the kingdom of heaven was near. Luke records the words of Jesus that taught John was a watershed figure in kingdom history.

> The Law and the Prophets were proclaimed until John. Since that time, the good news of the kingdom of God is being preached, and everyone is forcing his way into it (16:16).

Jesus declared to those in his presence that the kingdom was in their midst (Luke 17:21). John baptized with water, but he predicted the kingdom would be here when Jesus began baptizing with the Holy Spirit (Matt 3:11). Jesus promised his disciples, "Some who are standing here will not taste death before they see the kingdom of God come with power" (Mark 9:1; Luke 9:27).

N. T. Wright explained,

---

[22]Bright, *The Kingdom of God*, 215-216.

This could only mean one thing: Israel was at last going to be redeemed, rescued from oppression. God's "Kingdom" wasn't a state of mind, or a sense of inward peace. It was concrete, historical, real.... The strange thing about Jesus' announcement of the Kingdom of God was that he managed both to claim that he was fulfilling the old prophecies, the old hopes, of Israel and to do so in a way which radically subverted them. The Kingdom of God is here, he seemed to be saying, but it's not like you thought it was going to be.[23]

Parables of the Kingdom

Matthew 13 records eight parables about the kingdom. Jesus began with the parable of the four soils. While the gospel must be broadcast until it covers the whole earth, not everyone will respond alike.

Mark 4:26-29 gives an added insight. "First the stalk, then the head, then the full kernel in the head" describes the progressive nature of the kingdom. Too often we insist on immediate results when we should have faith in the long-term growth of the kingdom.

In Matthew 13:24-30 both the good grain and the tares grow together until harvest. This truth is repeated in the parable of the dragnet (vv 47-50) where the angels sort the good fish from the bad at the end of the age. The teaching that the church will be raptured out *before* the end is at variance with this outline given by Jesus.

Jesus taught that the kingdom of heaven was like a mustard seed in vv 31-32. It has a small beginning, but a great

---

[23]Wright, *Who Was Jesus?* 94-100.

influence. Here the emphasis is on visible growth. Drawing from the depiction of Ezekiel 17:23 that Israel will become like a shoot which will grow into a great cedar which will provide shelter for birds of every kind, Jesus described the kingdom as beginning small, but having great influence and blessing.

The kingdom of heaven is also like yeast which works silently and slowly, but eventually permeates the whole world (Matt 13:31-35). Here the emphasis is on the inward, but pervasive influence of the kingdom. The imagery that this yeast worked its way through all the dough describes the triumph of the gospel as it diffuses itself through all the nations and points back to the promise made in Genesis 12:3, that spiritual blessing would come to all the families of the earth. John Jefferson Davis commented

> These images of dramatic growth recall the mysterious stone from heaven that grew into a great mountain (Dan. 2:35) and the miraculous river of water from the temple that increased in depth and width apart from all human agency (Ezek. 47:1-12). . . . Both parables describe the small and insignificant beginnings, the gradual progress, and the final marvelous increase of the church.[24]

The parables concerning the mustard seed, the yeast, the wheat and tares, and the dragnet all imply the presence of the kingdom. Yet they all have a future component.

---

[24]Davis, *Christ's Victorious Kingdom*, 49-51.

We Are Given Authority

It would be obvious that the kingdom of God had come when the power of God's Spirit drives out demons. Jesus said, "But if I drive out demons by the Spirit of God, then the kingdom of God has come upon you" (Matt 12:28). Luke recorded a similar statement, "But if I drive out demons by the finger of God, then the kingdom of God has come to you" (11:20).

The fact that Satan's kingdom is being invaded and his possessions are being carried off is proof that the kingdom of God has come (Matt 12:25-29). "In the mighty works of Jesus, the power of the Kingdom has broken into the world; Satan has met his match, The cosmic end-struggle has begun."[25]

Christ establishes his house, by pulling down Satan's house. This was accomplished in a two-step rescue operation. First the master of the house was bound. Satan was bound at the cross. He still has power and influence in the world, but God is in control and only allows him some much rope. Second, the master of the house is robbed of his hostages. This happens every time someone is born again.

In the fourth century Athanasius wrote,

> Since the Savior has come among us, idolatry not only has no longer increased, but what there was is diminishing and gradually coming to an end: and not only does the wisdom of the Greeks no longer advance, but what there is is now fading away: And demons, so far from cheating any more by illusions and prophecies and magical arts, if they so much as

---

[25]Bright, *The Kingdom of God*, 218.

dare to make the attempt, are put to shame by the sign of the Cross. And to sum the matter up: behold how the Savior's doctrine is everywhere increasing, while all idolatry and everything opposed to the faith of Christ is daily dwindling, and losing power, and falling. And thus beholding, worship the Savior "Who is above all" and mighty, even God the Word; and condemn those who are being worsted and done away by Him. For as, when the sun is come, darkness no longer prevails, but if any be still left anywhere it is driven away; so, now that the divine Appearing of the Word of God is come, the darkness of the idols prevails no more, and all parts of the world in every direction are illuminated by His teaching.[26]

The church has been given the keys of the kingdom and are to bind and loose on earth what has been bound and loosed in heaven (Matt 16:18-19; 18:18). With the key of declaration we announce the terms of salvation. With the key of discipline we protect those who have spiritual life. With the key of prayer we move the hand of God. Through prayer Satan can be bound because he was defeated at the cross. It is not necessary for Christ to physically return to earth to bind Satan since he has authorized his church to exercise his authority.

The Olivet Discourse

In the Olivet Discourse, recorded in Matthew 24, Mark 13, and Luke 21, Jesus answered questions surrounding his prophecy of the destruction of the temple. The destruction of

---

[26] Athanasius, *Incarnation of the Word*, §55; *NPNF2* 4:66.

the temple signified the fact that God's kingdom was no longer to be centered in Jerusalem. False Christs, war, famine, earthquake, persecution, and apostasy are not signs of the end of the world; they mark the end of the old covenant. Jesus also describes these events are the beginning of birth pains. These were the birth pangs of the kingdom and signified new life. There would be no such signs announcing the second advent (Matt 24:36-44).

Of the three accounts, only Matthew records a second and third questions: "What will be the sign of your coming and of the end of the age?" Obviously these events were connected in the minds of the disciples with the destruction of the temple. Today, we have relatively little interest in what has happened and therefore the entire discourse is often misinterpreted as answering future questions. Mark, at least up to 13:32, and Luke do not deal with the second advent. Matthew deals with the AD 70 destruction of Jerusalem and the second advent.

Jesus gives very specific instructions to those who would be living through the siege of Jerusalem. The early Jewish Christians took the warning of Jesus in Matthew 24:15-21 seriously and escaped Jerusalem before it fell. Over a million Jews lost their lives in the siege of Jerusalem. However, not one Jewish Christian died during the siege of Jerusalem. The Roman army had actually entered the temple in Jerusalem and caused desecration. Then for no apparent reason they withdrew. The Jews took this as a sign of weakness and pursued the retreating army. Both Josephus and Eusebius record that this gave the Christians an opportunity to escape the city. They fled to a rock fortress hidden in the hill country about sixty miles northeast of Jerusalem, called Pella.

Jesus concludes his answer to the first question by stating in Matthew 24:34 that the generation to whom he was speaking would not pass away until all these things have happened. While this seems to be the natural break in the text, what about vv 27-31? Which question do they answer?

Beginning with v 36 Jesus begins to answer the question regarding his return at the end of the world. Most of the material which follows (Matt 24:37-25:46) is only found in Matthew, because only Matthew deals with the remaining two questions: the sign of his coming and the end of the age. Unlike the specificity of the first 35 verses, the rest of Matthew 24 and chapter 25 become more general. Like other prophetic passages this passage leaves us with unanswered questions and moves into three illustrations which emphasize preparedness. Then we are told Christ will come in his glory to judge the world (Matt 25:31-46).

Christ warns that during the siege of Jerusalem some will declare that he has secretly returned. He explains that his coming will not be secret, but will be like lightning which flashes across the sky from east to west (Matt 24:27). This description does not place the second advent at that time, but compares the false predictions made to the true circumstances of his return.

Then in v 29 Jesus quotes from Isaiah 13:10; 34:4 where it describes the sun and moon darkened, stars falling and heavenly bodies shaken. Here Jesus draws from apocalyptic imagery. This citation from Isaiah, therefore, must be interpreted symbolically since it is given symbolically.

Peter gives much the same description in Acts 2:19-20 and there quotes from the apocalyptic language of Joel. Sun, moon, and stars symbolize nations. This precedent was set in Genesis 37:9. Even today the flags of many nations include the use of stars, moon and stars, moon and sun, or sun. Immediately after the fall of Jerusalem, "the lights went out" for Israel as a nation as the kingdom of God was taken away from them (Matt 21:43).

The statement made in Matthew 24:30 that at that time "the sign of the Son of Man will appear in heaven," does not refer to his second advent. Instead it corresponds to Daniel 7:13 which describes the ascension of Christ back to his heavenly throne.

> In my vision at night I looked, and there before me was one like a son of man, coming with the clouds of heaven. He approached the Ancient of Days and was led into his presence. He was given authority, glory and sovereign power; all peoples, nations and men of every language worshiped him. His dominion is an everlasting dominion that will not pass away, and his kingdom is one that will never be destroyed.

Jesus did not tell his disciples that he would appear in the *sky*. Literally he said he would appear in heaven and those on earth would see a sign that proved he was in heaven, sitting at the Father's right hand. According to Acts 2:30-36 his giving of the Holy Spirit at Pentecost is that sign.

All the tribes of the land of Judea will mourn the destruction of Jerusalem (Zech 12:12) as they see him coming in judgment upon them. The sequence of Matthew 24:29-31 describes the destruction of Jerusalem and the shake down of the world powers. Then the nations begin to recognize Christ as king and the gospel will spread to all nations as his messengers sound the gospel trumpet calling all nations into the kingdom.

"This gospel of the kingdom will be preached in the whole world," we are told in v 14, "and then the end will come." Here Jesus anticipates the final two questions concerning his return and the end of the world which he will return to at v 36. Matthew 28:19-20; Acts 1:6-8; 2 Peter 3:10-12 all make a similar point; the nations must be discipled before Christ returns.

Yes, Christ will return at the end of the world to judge the nations, but he will only return after the gospel has been preached to the world. Richard Watson believed that the end "cannot arrive until all flesh has seen the salvation of God, through the publication of Christianity."[27] Those who follow Christ must endure to the end. No early rapture is promised.

At the end of human history when Christ returns there will be a general resurrection. Those who belong to Christ, whether living or dead, will be caught up to meet the Lord in the air. However, this is not a secret rapture which occurs prior to the second advent. The resurrection and rapture are two aspects of one event in which all the dead are raised and the Christians are gathered unto Christ.

Later that same evening Jesus explained to his disciples that it was better that he depart, return to heaven, and send the Holy Spirit (John 16:7). If the Holy Spirit is the one who brings souls into the kingdom through the new birth, why teach that the kingdom cannot come until Christ physically returns?

The Defeat of Satan

Three times John called Satan "the prince of this world" (John 12:31,14:30, 16:11). This simply means that Satan is ruler over the domain of darkness, not that Satan owned or ruled God's creation. "The whole world is under the control of the evil one" (1 John 5:19). Greg Bahnsen concluded that

---

[27]Watson, *Exposition*, 261.

this world and *this age* both denote the immoral realm of disobedience against God, the life of man apart from God, the ethical sphere which is antagonistic to God — rather than geographic and temporal spheres. While "this age" and "this world" are found in space and time, they are not fundamentally spatio-temporal entities. They are the spiritual kingdom of darkness.[28]

Jesus declared, "My kingdom is not of this world" (John 18:36). Separating the church from the world system under Satan is necessary, but Jesus never suggested that his kingdom was not *in* this world.[29]

Darkness and ignorance had spread across the earth and Satan could claim it was his since God put man in charge and man fell under the bondage of Satan. Although the earth always belonged to God (Ps 24:1), this legal claim against it was settled at the cross. In anticipation of this victory Jesus declared, "The prince of this world now stands condemned" (John 16:11). At the cross Satan received a death blow to his head from which he will never recover (Gen 3:15). Christ came to destroy the devil's work (1 John 3:8) and it was by his death that he set us free (Heb 2:14-15).

Revelation 12 describes war in heaven (vv 7-9). Sometime in the distant past, prior to Genesis 3, Satan was cast down to earth (v 4). Satan fell because he rejected truth (John 8:44). Pride brought the devil under judgment (1 Tim 3:6). God did not spare the angels when they sinned (2 Pet 2:4).

---

[28]Bahnsen, "The Person, Work, and Present Status of Satan," 26.

[29]Gregg, *Empire of the Risen Son*, 1:22.

Apparently some fallen angels have been bound ever since (Jude 6). However, if a third of the angels fell, there are twice as many good angels as bad ones.

Satan experienced a second defeat at the cross. We can pinpoint the point in time when his second defeat occurred by observing the convergence of several events mentioned in this text. Satan attempts to prevent the birth of the Messiah (Rev 12:4b), but the ruler is born.

The next event mentioned is the ascension (v 5b). Since Satan can no longer attack the Messiah, he turns on the church (v 13). Satan's second defeat was the time when salvation was completed and the kingdom of God was established (v 10). The triumph over Satan was connected with the shed blood of the Lamb (v 11). It was also the time when the persecution of the early Church began (v 12). As a result of this second defeat Satan lost all standing in heaven (v 8). He could no longer accuse the saints like he did with Job (Job 1:6; 2:1; see also 1 Kgs 22:19-22; Zech 3:1). In anticipation of this Jesus said, "I saw Satan fall like lightning from heaven" (Luke 10:18).

Satan is filled with fury because he knows that his time is short (v 12). He is facing his third and final defeat. This drives him to persecute the church. But those within the kingdom continue to progressively overcome Satan through the blood of Jesus Christ. "Pleading the blood" is not a magical phrase. It implies the concept that if God has redeemed us, Satan has no legal claim over us. If God has sprinkled us by his blood, he owns us and we are a "people belonging to God" (1 Pet 1:2; 2:9). When Satan attacks us, he will have to deal with the God to whom we belong.

Like a squatter who claim territory he does not own, Satan will take every foothold we allow him to possess. But he has no legal authority. We are not to allow the devil to gain a foothold (Eph 4:27). We are to tear down strongholds and take captive every thought to make it obedient to Christ (2 Cor 10:4-5). If we resist Satan he will flee from us (Jas 4:7).

At the death of Jesus, he descended into the realm of death. He preached to the spirits in prison (1 Pet 3:19) proclaiming his victory. The underworld (*sheol* in Hebrew and *hades* in Greek) was divided into two parts — the realm of punishment and the region of reward. Jesus entered into the realm of hell and disarmed "the powers and authorities, he made a public spectacle of them, triumphing over them by the cross" (Col 2:15).

After binding Satan, Jesus threw open the doors of the other section and led captives out. This region of reward was referred to by the Jews as "Abraham's bosom." The righteous dead of the Old Testament could not enter heaven until Christ had purchased their redemption on the cross. David had written, "When he ascended on high, he led captives in his train and gave gifts to men" (Ps 68:18). Paul explained to the Ephesians,

> What does "he ascended" mean except that he also descended to the lower, earthly regions? He who descended is the very one who ascended higher than all the heavens, in order to fill the whole universe (Eph 4:8-10).

In the Roman culture when a general conquered, he would lead the defeated army through the streets of Rome in a victory celebration. Christ demonstrated the establishment of his kingdom by leading a defeated Satan in a parade through the region of death. Martin Luther expressed the victory of Christ.

I believe he descended into hell to overthrow and take captive the devil and all his power, guile and wickedness, for me and for all who believe in Him, so that henceforth the devil cannot harm me; and that He has redeemed me from the pains of hell, and made them harmless.[30]

The Kingdom and Pentecost

After his resurrection, Jesus gave many convincing proofs that he was alive. He appeared over a period of forty days and spoke about the kingdom of God (Acts 1:3). His kingdom was not postponed. Contrary to the Jewish mindset, the kingdom was not to be restored to Israel (v 6). Although the disciples asked, "Lord, will you at this time restore the kingdom to Israel?" Jesus does not directly answer their question, which revealed an implied Jewish nationalism. Instead, the disciples of Jesus were to go from Jerusalem to the ends of the earth (v 8).

The use of Joel 2:28-32 in Acts 2:15-21 demonstrates how prophetic imagery can apply to historical events. Peter explained that the day of Pentecost was the fulfillment of Joel's prophecy and that we are now in the last days. "Blood and fire and billows of smoke" refers to the calamities that fell upon Jerusalem at the time of its destruction in AD 70.

At Mount Sinai, when the law was given, the earth shook (Exod 19:18). Pentecost was the commemoration of the giving of the law. At Pentecost God shook the whole world. David Chilton explained that Peter is describing the establishment of Christ's kingdom by bringing together theologically two events: the outpouring of the Holy Spirit and the destruc-

---

[30]*Works of Martin Luther*, 2:371.

tion of Jerusalem. The generation from Pentecost to the first-century holocaust saw the conclusion of the old covenant and the beginning of the new covenant.[31]

In his Pentecostal sermon Peter links the resurrection, the ascension, and the outpouring of the Holy Spirit all as evidence that Christ's kingdom has begun (Acts 2:32-36). When the Holy Spirit was given on the day of Pentecost, Peter declared this was confirmation that Christ was seated on his throne and the worldwide kingdom of God had begun. Three times in Acts 2 there is reference made to the position of Christ at God's right hand (vv 25,33,34). He is both Lord and Christ (2:36); ruler and Savior (Acts 5:31). The gift of the Holy Spirit (Acts 2:33) and the gifts of the Spirit are the result of Christ's ascension and session (Eph 4:8).

Pentecost affirms the resurrection for those of us who did not see the risen Christ in the flesh. Pentecost inaugurated the kingdom of Christ. The language division at Babel was reversed at Pentecost. To the extent that we preach the one book, the church has a common language and a united voice. Wesley famously declared, "O give me that book! At any price, give me the book of God!"[32]

Pentecost empowers us for world evangelism. We are representatives of Christ and in his Name we are to resist and bind Satan, as well as preach the gospel, making disciples of all nations. The authority Adam lost has been restored to the church and the gates of hell cannot overcome the church (Matt 16:18).

Pentecost gives hope for world revival. If Pentecost was the former rain predicted by the prophets of old, then there

---

[31] Chilton, *Paradise Restored*, 100-101.

[32] Wesley, Preface to Standard Sermons, ¶ 5.

must also be a later rain. Between the former and later rain we can have frequent seasons of refreshment (Acts 3:19). John Fletcher wrote, "We can patiently and confidently expect those times of refreshing which shall assuredly come from the presence of the Lord looking forward to that promised restitution of all things."[33]

Kingdom Prosperity

In Romans 11 Paul uses the analogy of the olive tree. Those branches which are cut off represent apostate Israel. The wild branches which are grafted in represent the gentiles. However, there is only one tree. God does not have two covenant peoples.

Romans 11:25-26 predicts that after the full number of the gentiles has come in, all Israel will be saved. God has not abandoned Israel. Those who believe will be grafted back into the tree (vv 1-24). John Wesley expected this as part of the general spread of the gospel.[34]

There will be a "vast harvest among the heathen." The resulting prosperity will provoke the Jews to jealousy. *Jealousy* occurs in Romans 10:19; 11:11, 14 to describe the desire stirred among the Jews when they contrast their present state alongside the prosperity of the converted pagans. This is also depicted in Zechariah 8:23. The early Methodists believed the gospel would have already been received by the Muslims and

---

[33]Fletcher, *Works*, 3:165.

[34]Wesley, "The General Spread of the Gospel," Sermon #63, ¶25.

pagans if they had conversed with real Christians.[35] The inference is that the Jews would have already been converted, as well, if the nominal church had its act together.

The Jewish people as a whole will be converted "being convinced by the coming in of the Gentiles. But there will be still a larger harvest among the Gentiles, when all Israel is come in."[36] The conversion of both Jews and Gentiles will take place through the preaching of the Gospel. Both Jew and Gentile will belong to the one Church of Jesus Christ and Israel will not be restored as the kingdom. Instead, the whole world will become the kingdom of God (Rev 11:15).

Victory in the Book of Revelation

Some prophecy buffs give the impression that we can decode anything we want to know about the future from this book. Yet this is not primarily a book about the future. Kenneth Gentry wrote, "The closer we get to the year 2000, the farther we get from the events of Revelation."[37] The very first verse of the book establishes the time frame. The revelation is of things which *must soon take place*. Twelve more times throughout the book either one of two subjects are said to be *soon* — the unfolding of this book and the coming of Christ.

The unfolding of the message of Revelation is not primarily events which occur at the second advent of Christ, but which occur during the first century. Of course, future events are also referred to, but they are not said to be *soon*.

---

[35]Coke, *Commentary*, 6:127. Wesley, *Notes*, 394; Benson, *Notes*, 5:95.

[36]Direct quotes in this paragraph are from Wesley, *Notes*, 395.

[37]Gentry, "A Preterist View of Revelation," 37.

There is nothing in this book to frighten us; there is plenty in this revelation to empower us. We are not victims; we are victors. If God could take a group who were meeting behind locked doors after Jesus died and so transform their outlook that they turned their world upside down, then the lesson we are to learn is that the church of Jesus Christ cannot be stopped.

The early followers of Jesus could not fully grasp his deity, his majesty, his authority. They were surprised by the resurrection power they witnessed at Easter. Then they were overwhelmed by the baptism with the Holy Spirit at Pentecost. With their confidence based on the resurrection of Christ and the outpouring of the Spirit, they set out to evangelize the world.

But now nearly a generation had passed since Pentecost and their confidence was waning. They had been scattered and hunted down. They had been betrayed by their Jewish brothers, persecuted by the Roman government, and many, like Stephen, had become martyrs. By now all of the original apostles had been executed except for John. It had cost them everything to identify with Jesus Christ. They had been rejected by their families, thrown out of the synagogues, barred from the trade guilds, counted as traitors by the Roman government because they would not say "Caesar is Lord." The Hebrew writer had to deal with the issue of discouragement. There was a temptation to go back to all they had left and give it up. Apparently some did renounce Christ and became apostates.

The early church also was asking, if Jesus Christ is really Lord and has established a kingdom that will cover the earth, why were they beaten around like a band of renegades? This question was stated in 6:10, "How long, Sovereign Lord, holy and true, until you judge the inhabitants of the earth and avenge our blood?"

John himself was banished to a lonely island, when Christ breaks through with this message of hope for the church. This is the revelation of Jesus Christ. In this revelation the curtains are parted and his followers see his deity, his majesty, and his authority like they have never seen him. They are assured that he is on the throne, he is in control, and everything is running right on schedule. They understand that in the spiritual realm there is a cosmic struggle taking place. Satan had usurped authority over this earth, but the legality of who owned this world and who was the legitimate master of the human race was settled on the cross. Now the kingdom of God was moving like a mighty steam roller and these dejected followers of Christ were guaranteed victory. But things would get worse before they got better. As the gospel was preached, strongholds were being brought down, Satan was being routed, the kingdom of God was becoming established — but not without one tremendous, final struggle from the forces of darkness.

They were in the middle of the great tribulation. Jesus had foretold that there had never been anything like it and it would never be equaled again (Matt 24:21). These early followers of Jesus Christ did not need to be told that the devil was trying to destroy them before they got the gospel seed planted. They knew they were under an all-out assault. But the spiritual significance of this assault was explained to them in John's message through the use of symbolism. They were promised triumph through tribulation. Christ repeatedly assured them that he was coming soon to judge their oppressors. The struggle may be severe, but the victory of the Christ's kingdom "is at no time in doubt. The battle has already been won at Calvary."[38] These were the birth pangs of a new creation.

We must grasp three eschatological concepts:

- the decisive victory of Christ at the cross
- the progressive victory of Christ across history
- the final victory of Christ at his second advent.

The emphasis of Revelation 19 is on the progressive victory of Christ across history. On the robe of Christ is written "King of Kings and Lord of Lords." But this description was preceded by a statement that Christ "treads the winepress of the fury of the wrath of God Almighty." Isaiah 63 depicted the Savior with his garments stained crimson. Calvary was the winepress where he shed his blood to turn away God's wrath. Christ trod the winepress alone (v 3) because salvation is through no other. In Revelation 7:14 our robes are washed and made white in his blood. However, as our High Priest, his robe will always be stained. The same robe that declares his kingship is also stained with blood. Again the Scriptures tie the kingdom of Christ to his victory at the cross.

The cross was the turning point in redemptive history. A universal atonement is the basis of universal hope. Ultimately, all things will be reconciled to Christ and he will have dominion over everything (Col 1:18-20). The universal atonement of the last Adam not only counteracts the universal sentence of death incurred by the first Adam, but the victory of Christ is superabundant, restoring much more than was ever lost (Rom 5:20). While everyone will not be saved, the race as a whole will be redeemed. Mankind as a race will be saved. However, this concept of redemption accomplished does not

---

[38]Bright, *The Kingdom of God*, 241.

imply universalism, the annihilation of those who are not redeemed, nor the salvation of a mere remnant who alone are elect.[39]

At Asbury Theological Seminary is a mural in the administration building. It depicts Christ riding across the sky on his white horse with a blaze of light emanating from his hand. On earth beneath, John Wesley is also on horseback and reaches upward to receive the divine touch. That spark is transferred across the Atlantic Ocean to Francis Asbury and Henry Clay Morrison, the founder of the seminary. The symbolism is obvious; it is a depiction of Revelation 6 and 19. Christ does not return somewhere in chapter 19. Those who interpret the second coming of Christ in Revelation 19 see the millennium as a future period, often teaching the reestablishment of a Jewish kingdom. But the horse and his rider often appear in the sky and when the general in the saddle executes his battle strategy on planet earth, history is again altered and his kingdom leaps forward.

Revelation 20 described the kingdom as a reign of a *thousand years*. Rob Staples observed that while the images in the book of Revelation are generally understood in a symbolic or metaphorical sense, most millennialists inconsistently take the *thousand years* in a literal sense. Apparently the writer of Revelation did not have a number higher than one thousand. When he wished to express a greater number he writes 'thousands upon thousands and ten thousand times ten thousand' (5:11). Staples concluded that what is meant by the term *thousand* in Revelation 20 may simply be "our future in Christ. . . . It will be magnificent, and it will be forever."[40]

---

[39]Pope, *Compendium*, 3:427-447.

[40]Staples, "Millennium," 32.

Robert Mulholland agrees that "biblically, the largest conceivable unit of time was a thousand years." This is confirmed by the awkward usage in Ecclesiastes 6:6 of living "a thousand years twice over." Mulholland believes the millennium is "a great period of history that began with the Cross and Resurrection and ends with the consummation of God's victory." He observed that the phrase *thousand years* occurs without the definite article in 20:2,4 and in the remaining instances where a definite article is used (vv 3,5,6,7) it is a reference back to the same subject previously introduced. Therefore, the emphasis is not upon a precise period of time, but upon the quality of the time.[41] Therefore, the *millennium* is symbolic language for the kingdom of Christ which exists between Christ's first and second advent. Christ returns *after* this "thousand years," to raise the dead and judge the world.

There are also two resurrections taught in Revelation 20 — spiritual and physical. When Christ returns there will be a general resurrection, which is described in v 13. John 5:24-29 brings together in one statement both spiritual and physical resurrection. Spiritual resurrection *has now come* and *a time is coming* when physical resurrection will occur.

The *first resurrection* (Rev 20:5) refers to our entrance into the kingdom. Through the new birth we share in the resurrection life of Jesus Christ. We are composed of both body and spirit. According to Ephesians 2:1 we were dead in our trespasses and sin when God gave life to the spirit in the new birth. Everyone who has ever come to spiritual life has experienced *the first resurrection* and reigns with Christ (Eph 2:6). They are *blessed and holy* (v 6) and will be raised bodily to eternal life.

John gave hope to the early church. John recorded the cry

---

[41] Mulholland, *Revelation*, 307-308.

of the martyrs in 6:10 and here he explains that even though they were persecuted and beheaded for their testimony, they had resisted the beast of Rome. Now they were actually given authority to sit with Christ in the heavenlies and to reign with him a thousand years.

The church consists of those who have already received a spiritual resurrection. The church lives on and reigns both on earth and in heaven. The saints advance God's kingdom on earth; even the martyrs who died become God's triumphant army in heaven and are alive with Christ. Revelation 20:4-6 explains that it does not matter whether the church is in heaven or on earth, they are reigning with Christ. John was playing with the concept of two deaths and two resurrections. No doubt what he has in mind was the teaching of Jesus which he recorded in John 5:24-29.

His kingdom comes as people experience the new birth and exercise their spiritual authority to bind Satan. Since the result of Satan being bound is that he can not deceive (v 3), this suggests that he is bound through the truth of the gospel. Therefore, v 4 describes the church in heaven and on earth exercising her spiritual authority. Satan is bound in this present age through the power of the cross as the victory of Christ's resurrection is enforced by the followers of Christ. Greg K. Beale wrote that

> the binding and the millennium are best understood as Christ's authority restraining the devil in some manner during the church age. This means that the restraint of Satan is a direct result of Christ's resurrection. If so, the binding, expulsion, and fall of Satan can be seen in other NT passages that affirm with the same terms that the decisive defeat of the

devil occurred at Christ's death and resurrection.[42]

The Hope of the Gospel

Mankind was created to rule this earth for God (Gen 1:28). As the last Adam, dominion has been restored to Christ (1 Cor 15:27; Heb 2:8). This is the *new* creation of Isaiah 65.

Our dominion has been restored by Christ in "the new man" in order to complete God's purpose in history. Greek has two words for "new" — *neos* and *kainos*. The "new man" in Ephesians 2:15 is new in quality and kind, not just new in point of time. Both Jew and Gentile are to be incorporated into *one new man* (Eph 2:15).

Christ is our basis of unity and he has destroyed the divisions through the cross (Eph 2:14, 16). Grace closed the chasm. The cross settles everything. He himself is our peace. Peace (*shalom* in Hebrew) is more than a cessation of hostilities; it denotes positive well being and salvation and is the gift of God. Peace is embodied in Christ. He is the prince of peace (Isa 9:6). He is our peace offering reconciling us with God; he makes peace reconciling us with each other.

Psalm 2:8 promises the nations as the inheritance of Christ. Christ died for the whole race and there will be an innumerable host in heaven from every nation, language, and culture (Rev 5:11, 7:9-10). These people will be saved in this life, and their conversion will have an impact upon this world. Romans 11:26 promises "all Israel will be saved." What an impact this conversion will make on the world! Habbakuk 2:14, Zechariah 9:10 and other Old Testament prophecies foresaw a golden age upon earth.

In Matthew 6:10 Jesus instructed us to pray "your king-

---

[42]Beale, *NIGTC* , 985-988.

dom come on earth." Thomas Oden explained, "The reign of God is present wherever God's will is done."[43] Although the kingdom began at Pentecost, there must be a future aspect or there is no longer any need to pray this petition.

Colossians 2:15 teaches that Christ triumphed at Calvary and the church is commissioned to conquer through his authority. The gospel has the power to change society (Matt 16:19).

But we don't live long enough to see God work at this level. Iain Murray described the Puritan hope, a century before it was picked up by the early Methodists.

> The success of the gospel for which they yearned was bound up with their trust in Christ. They never gave way to the feeling that because the condition of the world was so deplorable the Second Coming of Christ was the only hope for mankind; in their mind, to have done so would have been to fall into unbelief in regard to the promised results of his first coming. If what was predicted seemed impossible, the remedy was to contemplate more closely the authority and glory which now belongs to the Head of the Church.
>
> Christians in their successive generations are but one agency in the hands of God, and for the Puritan, with his long-term view, it concerned him little whether he was called to sow or to reap; what mattered was that the final outcome is certain. So persecution could be faced; or the appalling darkness of entirely non-Christian nations. For the men of this noble

---

[43] Oden, *Life in the Spirit*, 284.

school neither promising circumstances nor immediate success were necessary to uphold their morale in the day of battle.[44]

Kenneth Scott Latourette divided church history into seven segments.

- During the first five centuries, Christianity won the professed allegiance of the large majority of the population of the Roman Empire.

- Between AD 500-950 Christianity suffered the greatest losses which it has ever encountered. It's very existence was threatened. Yet even during this decline, the gospel advanced geographically to new regions.

- This reversal was followed by four centuries of advance.
- Between AD 1500-1750 a series of awakenings revitalized the Christianity of Western Europe and missionaries carried Christianity to a larger portion of the earth than had ever been evangelized previously.

- Latourette called the period from AD 1750-1815 a *pause*. However, while menaced by a series of events and movements, there were few actual losses, and new movements would later advance Christianity to a new high level of vigor.
- From AD 1815-1914 the faith was threatened by forces which were openly or tacitly hostile to Christianity. But new life in Christianity swelled to a flood.

---

[44]Murray, *The Puritan Hope*, 90, 235.

- The last period which Latourette surveyed began with AD 1914 and continued into the mid-twentieth century.

He concluded that Christianity has become the most potent single force in the life of mankind. In a supplemental chapter, Ralph Winter concluded that "by 1975 Christianity had clearly outpaced and was continuing to outgrow all other religious movements in global size and influence."[45]

When Israel moved into the promised land, God said he would go before them and drive out their enemies. But he explained that he would not do it all at once.

> I will not drive them out in a single year, because the land would become desolate and the wild animals too numerous for you. Little by little I will drive them out before you, until you have increased enough to take possession of the land (Exod 23:29-30).

In a similar way, the kingdom of Christ advances in a similar way. Hebrews 12:28 not only teaches that this kingdom cannot be shaken, but that it advances progressively. They were already receiving it in the first century and the present passive participle *we are receiving* implies progressive expansion, not a crisis inauguration, at the second advent. Wiley wrote that this kingdom cannot be shaken because God has established it, and of the increase of his kingdom there shall be no end.[46]

---

[45]Latourette, *History of Christianity*, 1:xxii-xxiv, 270, 275; 2:xii, 995, 1506.

[46]Wiley, *Epistle to the Hebrews*, 409.

Even if the curse is progressively lifted as the kingdom expands, it will never be completely lifted because the population will still die during the millennium (Isa 65:20; Zech 8:4-5). In Isaiah's description, the kingdom of God on earth has produced a new world but not a perfect world. Sin, crime, disease, and death will not be eradicated in this world.

While we cherish the hope of heaven, there is reason for Christian optimism here on earth. If we love our neighbor as ourselves, we cannot escape our responsibilities here. We must be heavenly minded as well as salt and light here on earth.

If we again turn to the doctrine of personal salvation, many people stop far short of all that God has provided. The same shortcoming exists corporately. The poisonous pessimism of dispensationalism tells us that the kingdom of Christ has been postponed and that we are living in a Laodicean age. We see the world through our subjective circumstances. Often it is those who enjoy the most blessing who complain the loudest about how bad things are. Those who declare the world is worse now than ever before simply have no grasp of world history. Yet across history the influence of this kingdom has already elevated the status of women and abolished slavery. It has cared for the handicapped, built hospitals and orphanages, taught people to read and given them an education, and raised the standard of living.[47]

While some doctrinal systems teach that "miserable

---

[47] Schmidt, *Under the Influence: How Christianity Transformed Civilization* (2001); Garlow, *How God Saved Civilization* (2000); Tennent, *How God Saves the World* (2017); Hudson, *How Jesus Changed the World* (2016); Hill, *What Has Christianity Ever Done for Us?* (2005); D'Souza, *What's So Great About Christianity?* (2007).

Christianity," epitomized in Romans 7, is the best we can hope for, the opposite error is human perfection void of saving grace. At the cosmic level, the choice is not between a gnostic view that this world is hopeless or that we can build utopia through government programs.

Enlightenment philosophy denied man's fallen nature and relied upon the sufficiency of human reason. Thus, for them the "kingdom" is a product of our activity. This counterfeit view rejects the supernatural character of Christ's kingdom.

Evolutionary theory, as applied to human history, represented man as gradually growing into perfection. Thus, the counterfeit kingdom would be established on earth gradually as man evolved.

The concept of a secular utopia, financed through state spending programs, may be a vestige of Christian influence among liberal politicians; but the only common element between a secular utopia and historic postmillennialism is that both worldviews are hopeful.[48] However, the old humanistic notion that big government can legislate human progress is a false hope.

Our hope is a big God who has a master plan for victory. Liberal optimism that a better world will arrive through education, social reform, and legislation cannot honestly be equated with a conservative, Bible-based optimism that the Holy Spirit will bring a worldwide revival in which people turn from sin in repentance, receive the Spirit in regenerating power, and submit to God's law as a way of life. Therefore, let us make his kingdom our first priority.

It is quite possible that I am wrong at some point in my understanding of eschatology and the biblical sequence of

---

[48]See Berkhof, *Systematic Theology*, 718-719; Quandt, "The Secularization of Postmillennialism," 390-409.

events. However, Scripture is full of hope and we must not abandon the hope that Christ's kingdom will prevail, regardless of the details.

William Arthur, (1819-1901) was secretary of the British Wesleyan Methodist Missionary society from 1851 to 1868. In his famous book *Tongue of Fire* he asked,

> Do we pray for the salvation of the lost and preach the gospel with a full expectation of doing no more than saving small companies of saints from amidst multitudes of sinners? When a little is accomplished it is looked upon as what the Gospel was sent to do? While we aim at few, we shall win but few since our success is proportional to our faith.

He argued that if we pray and work for the conversion of the world with the hope that the kingdom of God will one day cover the earth and if we find that our postmillennial optimism was in error, what harm has been done? We are simply found busy doing the work of the kingdom. But, on the other hand, if we believe that we are predestined to failure and that nothing can be done to advance the kingdom until Christ returns, and dispensationalism proves to be wrong, we have failed to carry out the great commission entrusted to us.[49]

King Jesus has directed us to do his business until he returns (Luke 19:15). We need not spiral into date-setting and eschatological speculation. All we need to know is that he will win the battle and that whatever we do to advance his crown rights is not wasted effort. "Always give yourselves fully to the work of the Lord, because you know that your labor in the Lord is not in vain" (1 Cor 15:58).

---

[49] Arthur, *Tongue of Fire*, 346-363.

BIBLIOGRAPHY

Arthur, William. *Tongue of Fire: or, the True Power of Christianity*. New York: Harper & Brothers, 1856.

Athanasius. *Selected Works and Letters: A Select Library of Nicene and Post-Nicene Fathers of the Christian Church*. Second Series. Vol. 4. Philip Schaff and Henry Wace, eds. 1891. Reprint, Grand Rapids: Eerdmans, 1978. [*NPNF*]

Augustine. *City of God. A Select Library of Nicene and Post-Nicene Fathers of the Christian Church*. First Series. Vol. 3. Philip Schaff, ed. Grand Rapids: Eerdmans, 1979.

Bahnsen, Greg. "The Person, Work, and Present Status of Satan." *The Journal of Christian Reconstruction* 1:2 (Winter 1974) 11-43.

Beale, Gregory K. *New International Greek Text Commentary: The Book of Revelation*. Grand Rapids: Eerdmans, 1999.

Benson, Joseph. *The Holy Bible, with Notes, All the Marginal Readings, Summaries, and the Date of Every Transaction*. 2nd ed. 5 vols. 1811-1815. Reprint, New York: Carlton & Phillips, 1856.

Berkhof, Louis. *Systematic Theology*. Grand Rapids: Eerdmans, 1941.

Binney, Amos and Daniel Steele. *The People's Commentary on the New Testament*. New York: Eaton &

Mains, 1878.
Bright, John. *The Kingdom of God*. Nashville: Abingdon, 1953.
Chilton, David. *Paradise Restored*. Tyler, TX: Reconstruction Press, 1985.
Clarke, Adam. *The Holy Bible, Containing the Old and New Testaments: The Text Carefully Printed from the Most Correct Copies of the Present Authorized Translations, Including the Marginal Reading and Parallel Texts; with a Commentary and Critical Notes, Designed as a help to a Better Understanding of the Sacred Writings*. 6 vols. 1811-1825. Reprint, Nashville: Abingdon, 1950.
Coke, Thomas. *A Commentary on the Holy Bible*. 6 vols. London: G. Whitfield, 1801-1803.
Davis, John Jefferson. *Christ's Victorious Kingdom*. Grand Rapids: Baker, 1986.
Edwards, Jonathan. *The Works of President Edwards*. Sereno Edwards Dwight and David Brainerd, eds. 10 vols. New York: Carvill, 1830.
_____. *Edwards on revivals: containing A faithful narrative of the surprising work of God in the conversion of many hundred souls in Northhampton, Massachusetts, A.D. 1735: also Thoughts on the revival of religion in New England, 1742, and the way in which it ought to be acknowledged and promoted*. New York: Dunning & Spalding, 1832.
Fletcher, John. *The Works of the Reverend John Fletcher*. 1833. Reprint, Salem, OH: Schmul, 1974.
Gentry, Kenneth L. Jr. "A Preterist View of Revelation," *Four Views on the Book of Revelation*, C. Marvin Pate, ed. Grand Rapids: Zondervan, 1998.
Gregg, Steve. *Empire of the Risen Son*. 2 vols. Maitland,

FL: Xulon, 2020.

Henry, Matthew. *Commentary on the Whole Bible*. 6 vols. 1712-1714. Reprint, McLean, VA: McDonald, 1980.

Kik, J. Marcellus. *An Eschatology of Victory*. Phillipsburg, NJ: Presbyterian and Reformed, 1971.

Latourette, Kenneth Scott. *A History of Christianity*. 2 vols. 1953. Reprint, Peabody, MA: Prince, 1997.

Lewis, C. S. *The Problem of Pain*. New York: MacMillan, 1962.

Luther, Martin. *Works of Martin Luther: An Anthology*. 6 vols. Philadelphia: Muhlenberg, 1943.

Mulholland, M. Robert Jr. *Revelation*. Grand Rapids: Francis Asbury Press, 1990.

Murray, Iain H. *The Puritan Hope*. Edinburgh: Banner of Truth, 1971.

Oden, Thomas C. *Systematic Theology, Volume Three: Life in the Spirit*. New York: HarperCollins, 1992.

Pope, William Burt. *A Compendium of Christian Theology*. 3 vols. London: Wesleyan Conference Office, 1880.

Quandt, Jean B. "Religion and Social Thought: The Secularization of Post-millennialism." *American Quarterly* 25:4 (Oct 1973) 390-409.

Reasoner, Vic. *A Fundamental Wesleyan Commentary on 1-2 Peter*. Evansville, IN: Fundamental Wesleyan, 2017.

_____. *A Fundamental Wesleyan Commentary on Hebrews*. Evansville, IN: Fundamental Wesleyan, 2025.

Spurgeon, Charles Haddon. *The Treasury of David*. 7 vols. 1870-1885. Reprint, Grand Rapids: Guardian Press, 1976.

Staples, Rob L. "Millennium," *Herald of Holiness* 87 (March 1998) 32.

Tozer, A. W. *The Knowledge of the Holy.* New York: Harper & Row, 1961.

Watson, Richard. *An Exposition of the Gospels of St. Matthew and St. Mark.* London: Wesleyan Conference Office, 1833.

Wesley, John. *Explanatory Notes Upon the New Testament.* 1754. Reprint, Salem, OH: Schmul, 1976.

_____. *The Bicentennial Edition of the Works of John Wesley.* Frank Baker and Richard P. Heitzenrater, eds. 26 vols. to date. Nashville: Abingdon, 1976-.

Wiley, H. Orton. *The Epistle to the Hebrews.* Kansas City: Beacon Hill, 1959.

Wright, Nicholas Thomas. *Who Was Jesus?* Grand Rapids: Eerdmans, 1993.

For Further Research

In 1999 my book *The Hope of the Gospel: An Introduction to Wesleyan Eschatology* was published. I read everything I could find, from every theological position, and began trying to work out a coherent system of eschatology. In this book I covered the major biblical passages, conflicting theological systems, the historical development of eschatology across church history, and a special emphasis on classic Methodist theology versus the shift that came within the American holiness movement. I closed the 416-page book with a practical, "so-what" conclusion.

Now, over a quarter century later, rather than write an updated second edition which tries to track everything written since my book, I have chosen to write a much more simple introduction. I would note that a student at Nazarene Theological College, Manchester, wrote his 2011 dissertation largely in response to my book. I also wrote *A Fundamental Wesleyan Commentary on Revelation*, first published in 2005. A second edition in two-volumes was published in 2023.

www.ingramcontent.com/pod-product-compliance
Lightning Source LLC
Chambersburg PA
CBHW060219050426
42446CB00013B/3113